Making Sense of
English in

Sex

Other titles in the series:

Making Sense of English Usage
Making Sense of Foreign Words in English
Making Sense of English in Money Matters
Making Sense of English in the Law
Making Sense of English in Religion
Making Sense of English in Alternative Medicine
Making Sense of English in Computers
Making Sense of English in Psychology

Making Sense of English in Sex

Lee McOwan

Chambers

Published 1993 by Chambers Harrap Publishers Ltd
43–45 Annandale Street, Edinburgh EH7 4AZ

A catalogue record for this book is available from the British Library

ISBN 0 550 18049 4

Typeset by Hewer Text Composition Services, Edinburgh
Printed in England by Clays Ltd, St Ives plc

Contents

Preface

We all know that sex can draw people together, but problems encountered, either individually or within a partnership, can also cause a lot of pain. At best sex enhances a loving relationship and brings the joy of a new life, but at worst it can kill – through disease, by lust murder, or by accident with the latest masturbation craze. Older children may be enticed by strangers to appear in a film or do some modelling, then find themselves the victims of pornographers or paedophiles. There has been much publicity about the abuse of young people in care, and 10 per cent of women interviewed in a recent survey claim to have experienced sexual interference within their own families. Almost every day there is another headline about AIDS and its fatalities, but at the same time it is currently estimated that only 3 per cent of young people in the south of England believe in saving sex for marriage. Approximately 40 per cent of sexually-active young women questioned admit to having had a sexual relationship before they reached 16. I therefore hope a little further knowledge about such subjects as auto-erotic asphyxia, high risk activities, incest, paedophilia, and sex therapy, will leave readers more enlightened, and better-equipped to make correct choices about their own sexuality. Those whose profession involves personal counselling will already be aware of the importance of being familiar with the terminology of sexual issues, but it hasn't always been easy to find concise information without sifting through a great deal of written material.

I haven't forgotten those whose main aim is the pleasure to be gained from a mutually loving relationship, and those whose desire is to conceive a child. This isn't designed as a self-help book, but I hope that some of the latest information on contraception, loving techniques, or infertility treatments will be of value to them. This book might also throw light on some of the physical problems that may be encountered by older men and women who enjoy, or would like to enjoy, their sexuality. And of course, like all the other books in the series, this one is tailor-made for those browsers who get their kicks from the English language. Indeed, it is the language which so often gets in the way, when people wish to develop an increased awareness of sexual issues. It is easy to glibly or jocularly use the terminology of sex; not so easy to be sure exactly what such terms mean. The knowledge of the relevant anatomical names is often not all it should be, and important medical, legal, or counselling implications can be neglected. Secondary school pupils, whose sex education can sometimes be fairly basic, and full of mythology, are a group I particularly had in mind when researching this book. But everyone is an ex-secondary school pupil, and myths and ignorance can live on, and – because of the potentially embarrassing nature of the subject matter – may never be resolved. My own four teenagers have been very tolerant of my predominantly sexual conversations while writing this book. They and their friends have taken an enormous interest in the project, for which I am grateful. I hope it will be of value to their age group, and enlighten them on the more complex aspects of sexuality.

Lee McOwan

Pronunciation Guide

Vowels

iː	need	/niːd/
ɪ	pit	/pɪt/
i	very	/ˈvɛri/
ɛ	pet	/pɛt/
æ	pat	/pæt/
ʌ	other	/ˈʌðə^{r}/
ʊ	book	/bʊk/
uː	too	/tuː/
u	influence	/ˈɪnfluəns/
ɒ	cough	/kɒf/
ɔː	ought	/ɔːt/
ɜː	work	/wɜːk/
ə	another	/əˈnʌðə^{r}/
ɑː	part	/pɑːt/

Glides

eɪ	plate	/pleɪt/
aɪ	sigh	/saɪ/
ɔɪ	ploy	/plɔɪ/
oʊ	go	/goʊ/
ɑʊ	now	/nɑʊ/
ɪə	hear	/hɪə^{r}/
ɛə	fair	/fɛə^{r}/
ʊə	poor	/pʊə^{r}/

Consonants

p	pit	/pɪt/
b	bit	/bɪt/
t	ten	/tɛn/
d	den	/dɛn/
k	cap	/kæp/
g	gap	/gæp/
ʃ	shin	/ʃɪn/
ʒ	pleasure	/ˈplɛʒə^{r}/
ʧ	chin	/ʧɪn/
ʤ	budge	/bʌʤ/
h	hit	/hɪt/
f	fit	/fɪt/
v	very	/ˈvɛri/
θ	thin	/θɪn/
ð	then	/ðɛn/
s	sin	/sɪn/
z	zones	/zoʊnz/
m	meat	/miːt/
n	knit	/nɪt/
ŋ	sing	/sɪŋ/
l	line	/laɪn/
r	rid	/rɪd/
j	yet	/jɛt/
w	quick	/kwɪk/

Other symbols

^{r} indicates an ‘r’ pronounced only before a following vowel

ˈ precedes the syllable with primary stress

Note

Words or phrases within an entry that are printed in **bold type** refer the reader to another entry where there is further relevant information. *Italic type* is used within entries to indicate significant related words that do not themselves have an entry (although they may have a cross-reference). Sources of words are also shown in italic type.

A

abortion

Termination of pregnancy before the foetus is capable of surviving outside the womb. In the UK, the legal limit for induced termination is 28 weeks from conception. Abortion can be performed by surgery or drug treatment but is a criminal offence unless allowed by the current Abortion Acts. Spontaneous or non-induced abortion is commonly known as **miscarriage**.

abuse (sexual)

Physical or emotional harm done to a child as a result of a sexual relationship with an adult. The incidence of sexual abuse of children within their own families has increasingly come to public attention in the 1980s and 1990s; some studies show that up to 10 per cent of women interviewed reported some form of sexual interference in their own childhood. The term can also be used generally with reference to adult victims, to describe molestation, incest, or rape.

See also **paedophilia**

adolescence

The transitional period between childhood and adulthood during which sexual maturity takes place. In Western culture this is commonly regarded as a difficult phase which young people and their parents have to endure. However, in Third World societies it is often given ritual recognition, eg in Sri Lanka when a girl has her first **period** she is made the figurehead of an elaborate ceremony, seated on a throne, and brought presents by friends and family.

adrenal androgens

Hormones which are thought to specifically trigger growth of underarm and pubic hair in male *and* female adolescents.

See also **androgen**

adultery

Sexual unfaithfulness of a husband or wife. In English law to commit adultery is one of the five factors individually regarded as leading to the irretrievable breakdown of marriage, constituting grounds for divorce.

age of consent

The age at which a girl may enter into a voluntary sexual relationship (which may or may not include intercourse), or an act which in other circumstances would be considered indecent assault. Currently the age of consent in Great Britain is 16, in Northern Ireland 17.

aging

The natural process of growing older, which can have physical effects on sexuality. For women from menopausal age, these may include gradual reduced vaginal lubrication and elasticity, and reduced intensity of orgasm. For men over approximately 50 years, there may be increased difficulty with erection and ejaculation. However, this is variable, and men and women who have remained sexually active without long periods of abstinence may have little decline in their libido or activity. See also **atrophic vaginitis; menopause**

AID

See **donor insemination**

AIDS

An acronym of *acquired immune deficiency syndrome*, the result of infection with a human immune deficiency virus (HIV). Groups at high risk are homosexual or bisexual men, persons with a history of intravenous drug abuse, sufferers from haemophilia, and individuals who have had casual sexual relationships, especially in sub-Saharan Africa, San Francisco, or New York, and their partners and offspring. Transmission is by direct blood or seminal contact and the virus slowly destroys the body's defence against infection. Mortality is high.

AIH

See **artificial insemination**

alcohol

See **aphrodisiac**

amenorrhoea /æmɛnə'ri:ə/

Absence of menstruation (in sexually mature, non-pregnant women) for more than 90 days, usually because of non-release of the egg from the ovary. There is such a wide range of possible reasons for this condition that a medical diagnosis should always be sought.

See also **anovulation**

anal intercourse

A form of sexual intercourse when thc penis penetrates the anus; also called *rectal intercourse*. It is common practice among homosexual males, and is considered a high risk activity. *Buggery* is anal intercourse between two men or a man and a woman. Known as sodomy in Scotland, it is a crime when it takes place between two men under the age of 21.

See also **sodomy**

androgen

A sex hormone necessary for the development of male genitalia in the foetus. During puberty, androgens are responsible for the development of secondary sexual characteristics, such as growth of the penis, testes, and pubic hair, the deepening of the voice, and muscular development.

anorgasmia

See **orgasmic dysfunction**.

anovulation

The lack of release of an egg from the ovary. This condition causes missed menstrual periods, or long cycles between menstruation.

See also **menstruation**

aphrodisiac

Any substance or potion thought to stimulate sexual desire and performance. The word *aphrodisiac* comes from Aphrodite, the Greek goddess of love who was reputed to have been able to lure any male. Over 500 aphrodisiacs have been recorded, though none has ever been proved to have a genuine aphrodisiac effect. Alcoholic drinks, especially gin, generally increase desire, but decrease performance.

See also **cantharides**; **mandrake**

areola /ə'ri:ələ/

The pink or brownish circle around the nipple. The term derives from the Latin diminutive of *area*, thus expressing the notion of a very small area.

See also **nipple**

arousal

A rather vague term meaning the bringing on of sexual excitement. It can be the result of skilled **foreplay** or seduction, or merely a fleeting thought or sight of something stimulating.

artificial insemination

The placing of semen in the vagina by means other than sexual intercourse, for the purpose of becoming pregnant. Carried out in infertility clinics, *AIH*, or *artificial insemination by the husband*, usually refers to the insertion of a husband's previously collected semen into his wife's vagina in circumstances where intercourse is impossible, perhaps because of disability or **impotence.**

See also **donor insemination**

artificial phallus

Any object of similar size and shape to an erect penis, used for sexual stimulation; also known as a *dildo*. Such devices vary greatly in sophistication, and include battery-operated vibrators with warmth and ejaculatory capacity. Some are used with a harness or made double-ended for use in lesbian

relationships. Masters and Johnson heralded the use of a see-through plastic phallus for research into what actually happens in the vagina during intercourse.
See also **clitoral stimulator**; **Masters**, **William H(owell)**; **vibrator**

atrophic vaginitis

The inflammation caused by the 'shrinking' of the vagina, when the lining of the vagina becomes thinner, drier and less elastic. The process is a normal consequence of aging due to the decreasing production of oestrogen hormones, and may occur in women of menopausal age and older. Treatment is with oestrogen drugs, either in the form of creams or tablets. The term derives from Latin ***atrophia*** 'lack of food or nourishment'.
See also **vaginitis**

autoerotic asphyxia

The deliberate reduction of oxygen to the brain to enhance orgasm; also called ***sexual asphyxia***. It is an extremely dangerous practice, using nooses, gags, etc, carried out by some young men while masturbating. It is estimated that up to 1 000 people die of sexual asphyxia each year in the United States. Recent research suggests that many so-called suicide victims may have been indulging in this practice, and their 'fail-safe' devices have failed.
See also **masturbation**

azoospermia

A total lack of **sperm** in the ejaculate. This may be caused by a blockage, and can often be surgically corrected.
See also **ejaculation**

B

bacterial vaginosis (BV)

A condition in which the balance between the different bacteria in the vagina is upset, causing a fishy odour. The cause is as yet unknown, and is not thought to be sexually transmitted, but products have recently come on the market to stabilize the acid balance and eliminate the smell.

balanitis

See **foreskin, infections of**

ballooning of the vagina

See **vasocongestion**

balls

See **testicles**

barrier method of contraception

Any of several methods of preventing pregnancy by trapping sperm at the point of ejaculation, or in the vagina, by means of an artifical barrier; sperm may also be deactivated with a chemical substance. The methods include the use of a condom on the penis, a diaphragm, cervical cap, or sponge in the vagina, or a spermicide used on its own, or with a condom or diaphragm. These methods involve careful preparation every time intercourse takes place, but if they are used correctly, the failure rates are nearly as low as those for the contraceptive pill. The barrier methods also reduce the risk of sexually-transmitted diseases.

See also **cervical cap**; **condom**; **contraceptive sponge**; **diaphragm**; **spermicide**

bestiality

Human sexual relationship with an animal; also known as

sodomy. It occurs mainly in farming communities, where men and women may attempt intercourse with ponies, calves, sheep, dogs, pigs, etc. Bestiality is against the law, and severe penalties can be imposed.
See also **sodomy**

bidet /ˈbi:deɪ/
An article of French bathroom furniture originally used for post-coital douching. It is now used commonly in Western countries for the washing of the genitals, anus, feet and anything else suited to its low height.
See also **douche**

bigamy
A criminal offence in the UK and most Western societies, occurring when someone who is already married enters into a 'marriage' with another person. If the previous marriage has been ended by divorce or death, or declared void, no offence has been committed.
See also **monogamy**; **polygamy**

birth control
See **contraception**

bisexual
A man or woman who has sexual relationships with people of the opposite sex as well as of the same sex. The term is not limited to persons who have an equal interest in both kinds of sex partner. For instance, homosexual individuals may marry for social reasons, while having a same-sex lover.
See also **homosexual**

blow job
See **oral sex**

blue balls
See **lover's balls**

body lice
See **pubic lice**

bonk
See **intercourse, sexual**

breasts
The milk-producing organs of the female reproductive system; also known as ***mammary glands***. Their secondary function is sexual. The breasts are regarded as a sign of femininity and eroticism by most societies, and are potentially two of a woman's most erogenous zones. In his book, *Joy of Sex* (1978, updated 1987 as *New Joy of Sex*), Alex Comfort succinctly describes the nipples as 'a direct hotline to her clitoris'. Only 1 per cent of women interviewed by **Masters** and **Johnson** reported orgasm as a direct result of breast stimulation, but most women experience, and 50 per cent enjoy, manual or oral stimulation of the breasts as part of the **foreplay** to intercourse.

From the health point of view, women must examine their breasts monthly for any changes, including discharge from the nipples, and lumps. About one in 20 women may develop breast cancer, and it causes over 10 000 deaths in England and Wales alone every year. Although the male breasts are a very immature version of the female breasts, they too are susceptible to the same diseases; but for every 100 women with breast cancer, it will occur in only one man.
See also **gynaecomastia**; **nipple**; **areola**

brothel
A place where prostitution is practised. Brothels are illegal in the UK and in America, except in Nevada where the law allows 'houses of ill-repute' in some areas. A brothel is defined as a place where two or more prostitutes offer their services; a call girl cannot be prosecuted for keeping a brothel if she works on her own. In the Middle Ages brothels were usually operated in public bath houses, and in Western countries now massage

parlours are often a cover for girls who offer sexual services to male clients after an initial introduction as a masseur.
See also **prostitute**

buggery
See **anal intercourse**

buttocks
The two lower, fleshy parts of the hip on which a person sits; more usually called the ***bottom***. It is arguably a major **erogenous zone** in both sexes, particularly visually. In apes the buttocks can be seen as a highly-coloured display.

BV
See **bacterial vaginosis**

C

call girl

See **prostitute**

candida

A form of yeast-stimulated **vaginitis** in women, which can be sexually transmitted; more popularly known as ***thrush***. Symptoms include itching, soreness, burning, pain with intercourse, and external discomfort when urinating. There is sometimes a discharge having the consistency of cottage cheese. The condition can be aggravated by wearing tight or nylon clothing. Treatment with antibiotics is usually successful, but there can be recurrences of infection in which case the man should be treated as well.

See also **vaginal infections**

cantharides /kæn'θærɪdi:z/

An **aphrodisiac** made from the horny outer case of the cantharides beetle, commonly known as ***Spanish Fly***. It is a lethal substance which has caused death on numerous occasions.

cap

See **diaphragm**

cassolette

The natural odour of a clean woman, especially when referring to the genital odour produced during love-making. The term is French, meaning 'perfume box'.

See also **pheromenes**

castration

The surgical removal of the testicles, causing sterility. Medical castration consists of giving a male a female sex hormone, and is

usually undertaken for the treatment of cancer of the prostate.
See also **eunuch**

celibacy

The state of living as an unmarried adult. Nowadays it commonly refers to the state of a person who has chosen to have no sexual relationships, either permanently or for a specific period of time. Examples include monks, nuns, and some feminists.
See also **chastity, virgin**

cervical cap

One of the barrier methods of birth control. The cervical cap is similar to the **diaphragm**, but fits tightly over the cervix and is held in place by suction. It is mainly used by women who are unable to use the diaphragm because of prolapse of the uterus.
See also **diaphragm**

cervical smear

A sample of tissue taken from the cervix to check for abnormal cells. If this is regularly done, cervical cancer can be caught in its early stages, and the risk of death much reduced. The process is also known as the ***Pap test***, an abbreviation of ***Papanicolaou test***, from Greek-born medical scientist George N(icholas) Papanicolaou (1883–1962), who devised it.
See also **cervix**

cervix

The neck of the womb. Its lower, blunt part projects into the vagina.
See also **Appendix; cervical smear**

chancre /ˈʃæŋkə/

A sore or lesion, usually on the genitals, painless, round and rubbery. It appears after exposure to syphilis.
See also **syphilis**

change of life
See **menopause**

chastity
The state of virginity or **celibacy**; also, continence, ie self-restraint in the matter of sexual appetite or bodily passions. The term derives from Latin ***castus*** 'pure'.

chemical barrier
See **spermicide**

chlamydia
A sexually transmitted disease (STD) causing damage to the reproductive tract, which may lead to infertility in men and women. It attacks more especially the **Fallopian tubes** in women. Chlamydia is difficult to detect because there are often no symptoms, but when symptoms do occur they are similar to other STDs and may disappear without treatment. American women are currently urged to have an annual test although it identifies only about 80 per cent of those infected. However, when positive, it is rarely wrong. As with many STDs, treatment of the male partner is encouraged.
See also **sexually transmitted disease**

chordee /'kɜ:di:/
A painful, inflammatory, downward curving of the erect penis. Chordee occurs when the urethra is shorter than the penis. This condition is often diagnosed at birth or during childhood, and can usually be surgically corrected.
See also **penis**; **urethra**

circumcision, female
A surgical operation to remove all or part of the clitoris, labia majora, and labia minora, as well as the narrowing of the vaginal entrance. There is no medical reason for this procedure, and the removal of female genitalia is considered barbaric in Western society. Female circumcision has been illegal since

1985 in Britain, but no prosecutions have been brought. Recent research estimated that up to 10 000 African girls living in Britain are at risk of being taken back to Africa for circumcision to comply with the traditions of their families. Human rights and feminist groups are working towards its ban worldwide, but many cultures regard it as a ritual sacrifice (performed without anaesthetic), as well as a means of ensuring virginity until marriage. Once widely practised in Somalia and the Sudan, the procedure has been illegalized there, but the custom remains throughout many non-European countries.
See also **clitorectomy**; **infibulation**; **masturbation**

circumcision, male
A surgical operation to remove the foreskin from the penis. It may be carried out for medical, cultural, or religious reasons. Male Jewish babies are circumcised eight days after birth, and Muslims insist on circumcision soon after birth, or definitely before marriage. Both cultures affirm that no male can gain entry to heaven uncircumcised. Children of certain other groups are circumcised just before or at puberty, as part of the initiation to adulthood. For instance, in Central Africa elaborate circumcision rites are usual, and in Asia a boy's **adolescence** is specifically marked by circumcision between the ages of 10 and 15. In Western society, routine circumcision of baby boys is now commonly regarded as inessential, as the foreskin normally retracts easily in an adult male. In males where the foreskin is too tight or there is infection through lack of hygiene, circumcision may be carried out in adulthood. There is no evidence of any difference in sensitivity during sexual intercourse between a circumcised or uncircumcised male.
See **Appendix**; **foreskin, infections of**; **smegma**

clap
See **gonorrhoea**

climacteric /klaɪˈmæktərɪk/
Pertaining to or constituting a critical period in human life; the

term derives from Greek 'critical point', literally 'rung of a ladder'. It is a technical and somewhat old-fashioned way of describing the menopause.
See also **menopause**

climax
See **orgasm**

clitoral hood
A tiny piece of tissue protecting the clitoris. Also called the *prepuce*, it is the fold of skin close to where the inner lips of the vagina meet and cover the clitoris. In a male embryo, the same tissue would develop into the foreskin.
See also **Appendix**; **clitoris**

clitoral stimulator
Any device used to rub against the woman's clitoris for sexual stimulation. Some are obtainable in the form of a rubber ring that fits round the base of a man's penis with a projection on the upper side.
See also **artificial phallus**; **clitoris**

clitorectomy
The surgical cutting out of a woman's clitoris; a type of female circumcision. It was performed, for instance, in the days when masturbation was thought to cause insanity and this was the cure. Now there are surgeons, particularly in America, who will remove the clitoral hood in an attempt to improve the ability to reach orgasm.
See also **circumcision, female**; **clitoris**

clitoris
The tiny button of tissue inside the opening of the vagina that is the equivalent of the man's penis. During sexual excitement it fills with blood and becomes relatively erect and swollen. It is the primary source of sexual pleasure for the woman and has no other function.

See also **Appendix**; **clitoral hood**; **clitoral stimulator**; **clitorectomy**; **penis**

coil
See **intra-uterine device**

coital orgastic dysfunction
The condition of being unable to reach orgasm during intercourse. Introduced by Masters and Johnson, the term has now been replaced by *anorgasmia*.
See also **Masters, William Howell**; **orgasmic dysfunction**

coitus /ˈkɔːtʊs/
Sexual intercourse of the penile-vaginal type. The term derives from Latin, meaning 'joining together'.
See also **intercourse, sexual**

coitus interruptus
The removal of the penis from the vagina before ejaculation, otherwise known as *withdrawal*. The term is Latin, literally meaning 'interrupted coitus'.
See also **coitus**; **onanism**

coitus saxonus
Sexual intercourse with clothes on, to protect from pregnancy. The term is from Latin *Saxonia* 'wool or cloth from the country of the Saxons'. It doesn't work.

come
See **ejaculation; orgasm**

conception
The fertilization of the ovum (egg), by a man's sperm, followed by implantation in the lining of of the uterus, leading to pregnancy.
See also **pregnancy**

condom

A disposable plastic or thin latex rubber sheath placed over the erect penis before intercourse. A **barrier method of contraception**, it also serves to give protection against sexually transmitted diseases, such as **AIDS**, and may be used with a spermicidal water-based cream. The term has a large number of slang or technical equivalents, such as ***French letter***, ***Johnny***, ***sheath***, ***prophylactic***, ***protective***, and ***rubber*** (American English). ***Female condoms*** are also now available. They are similar to male condoms, but used inside the vagina, where they are held with rings.
See also **spermicide**

contraception

The prevention of pregnancy by various artificial means when sexual intercourse takes place. Also called ***birth control*** or ***family planning***, it is now widely recognized as a useful method of population control, as well as protection against sexually transmitted diseases (with a barrier method). It has been opposed by the Roman Catholic Church for many centuries, and this church still prefers the 'natural' rhythm method, rejecting all others.
See also **barrier method of contraception**; **cervical cap**; **condom**; **contraceptive pill**; **contraceptive sponge**; **intra-uterine device**; **mini pill**; **rhythm method**; **sterilization**; **vasectomy**

contraceptive pill

A hormone pill which inhibits ovulation and acts as a form of contraception. It contains synthetic steroids similar to oestrogen and progesterone, and is taken for 21 days, followed by a 7-day interval during which menstrual bleeding occurs. Those who smoke and women over 40 should not use the contraceptive pill; the lower-dose pill is a safer alternative than the higher-dose one. Should a woman using the contraceptive pill experience severe abdominal, thigh, or chest pain, headaches, dizziness, shortness of breath, or loss or blurring of speech or vision, she must stop taking it immediately, and consult her doctor.
See also **contraception**; **mini pill**; **morning-after pill**

contraceptive sponge

A disposable foam sponge which has to be impregnated with spermicide, moistened with water, and inserted high into the vagina. It must be left in position for six hours after intercourse.
See also **contraception**

coprophilia

[Greek ***kopros*** 'dung' + ***philia*** 'friendship, love'] Sexual arousal from being rubbed with faeces, or from watching someone opening their bowels.
See also **paraphilia**

coquette

A flirt, usually female, who teases and arouses sexual feelings with no intention of responding to those feelings. The word is the modern feminine form of French ***coquet*** 'wanton, cocky'. The native English slang equivalent is ***prick-teaser***, describing someone who will not go 'all the way' or even part of the way.

coronal ridge

The ridge at the base of the glans (the head of the penis). In childhood the foreskin is attached to the coronal ridge and may not separate until adolescence.
See also **Appendix**; **penis**

crabs

See **pubic lice**

cremasteric reflex /krɛmə'stɛrɪk/

The capability of the testicles to withdraw hastily upwards in the scrotum in moments of danger or during sexual excitement. A drop in temperature will have the same effect.
See **scrotum**; **testicles**

cross-dresser

See **transvestite**

cruising
The American English slang term for driving around on the lookout for a sexual encounter, also called *kerb-crawling*. It usually refers to a man looking for the services of a prostitute, or a homosexual male in the search of a one-night stand.
See also **trick**

cryptorchidism
See **monorchism**; **testicles**

cuckold
An old-fashioned name for the husband of an unfaithful wife. The term derives from *cuckoo*, the metaphor suggesting that the man has been turned out of the nest.

cunnilingus
See **oral sex**

cunt
A vulgar term for a woman's external genital organs. In 1959 Penguin Books were prosecuted under the Obscene Publications Act for publishing D H Lawrence's novel *Lady Chatterley's Lover*, in which the word is used several times in the context of affectionate/erotic talk between the lovers during sexual intercourse. It is still one of the most forceful obscenities in the language, but has become more acceptable.
See also **vulva**

cystitis
An infection of the urinary tract causing a burning sensation. It is more common in women, and similar to *urethral syndrome* where the symptoms are caused by trauma to the **urethra** during intercourse.

D

D and C

The abbreviation for ***dilatation and curettage***, the scraping away of the lining of the uterus. This is performed in the treatment of heavy menstrual bleeding, after a **miscarriage**, and sometimes to terminate a pregnancy. It is usually carried out under a general anaesthetic.

de Sade, Marquis

See **sadism**

deviant behaviour

Sexual deviation.
See **paraphilia**

diabetes

As *diabetes mellitus*, a disorder of the process by which the body uses sugars and other carbohydrates, and in which insufficient amounts of the hormone insulin are produced. All sorts of sexual dysfunction in men and women may be caused by untreated diabetes, including erection problems, changes in ejaculation, inability to reach orgasm, and a reduction in sexual desire.

diaphragm

One of the **barrier methods of contraception**; also called a *cap*. It is a dome-shaped piece of latex rubber which has to be lubricated with spermicidal jelly and placed high in the vagina before intercourse. It should remain in place for six hours after intercourse. The correct size should be selected, and method of use should be demonstrated by medical staff at a family planning clinic. Unlike the condom, the diaphragm is re-usable, and will last up to two years if properly looked after.
See also **cervical cap**

dilatation and curettage
See **D and C**

dildo
See **artificial phallus**

diphallia /daɪˈfæliə/
The extremely rare condition of a male having two penises. Fewer than 80 cases have been recorded since the 17th century. Such defects can now be corrected early in a baby's life.

donor insemination
One of the choices for infertile couples when the man is infertile or carries a genetic disease; also called ***artificial insemination by a donor (AID)***. Frozen sperm from a bank of carefully screened donors is artificially inseminated into the woman's vagina. The couple should be given a medical history of the donor plus a list of his characteristics, but he will remain anonymous to them, as they will to him. Up to 60 000 healthy babies are born each year in America from donor insemination, and up to 80 per cent of women using the system become pregnant. The woman is able to have a normal pregnancy, and because the baby inherits the mother's genetic makeup, donor insemination is one of the most popular treatments for male infertility.
See also **artificial insemination**

douche /du:ʃ/
A method by which a cleansing agent such as water is forced into the **vagina** via a bag with a tube attached to it. Many myths about douching with all sorts of potions can be traced back as far as the 15th century, and even today about half of all women in America douche regularly in the name of personal hygiene. However, douching with any fluid may be harmful to the vagina, and will certainly decrease its ability to fight infection. Douching may also encourage sexually transmitted disease and pelvic inflammatory disease, and is NOT effective as a contraceptive measure since the sperm quickly move up into the cervix out of reach of the douche.

droit de Seigneur /drwɑ: də seɪnˈjɜ:/
The 'right of the master'; a French term describing the right of the Lord of the Manor to deflower the brides of his social inferiors. The term existed legally from feudal times as the 'right of the first night', from Latin *jus* **primae noctis**. In practice it appears to have been a threat to encourage the payment of marriage taxes, or else.

dry ejaculation
Another term for **retrograde ejaculation**.

dysmenorrhoea /dɪsmɛnəˈri:ə/
Cramp-like pains in the lower abdomen, experienced during **menstruation**. Most women suffer from at least mild dysmenorrhoea at some time in their life, usually early on, before childbirth.

dyspareunia /dɪspəˈru:niə/
Painful sexual intercourse, experienced by either men or women. For women the causes are numerous, and may include deep pelvic pain due to pelvic inflammatory disease, an ectopic pregnancy, ovarian cysts, endometriosis, or fibrous tumours. Pain around the genital area in either sex may be caused by cystitis, or sexually transmitted diseases, such as herpes, chlamydia, or gonorrhoea. Men may experience pain caused by phimosis, inflammation of the prostate gland, or chordee. Psychological problems such as vaginismus may result in pain on attempted intercourse.
See also **chlamydia**; **chordee**; **cystitis**; **ectopic pregnancy**; **endometriosis**; **foreskin, infections of**; **gonorrhoea**; **herpes**; **vaginismus**

E

ectopic pregnancy

A life-threatening condition for women when a pregnancy develops outside the womb, most usually in the **Fallopian tube**, or less usually in the ovary, cervix, or abdomen. An ectopic pregnancy might develop due to damage of the reproductive tract from sexually transmitted diseases, pelvic inflammatory disease, or as one of the side effects of pregnancy occurring while using the progestogen-only contraceptive pill (mini pill). Symptoms include severe lower abdominal pain, perhaps with vaginal bleeding. Should the surrounding tissue rupture, symptoms of shock will be apparent. Diagnosis is usually by means of ultrasound scanning or by the direct observation of the inside of the abdomen using a laparoscope, and is treated by the surgical removal of the foetus.

See also **mini pill**; **pelvic inflammatory disease**; **pregnancy**; **sexually transmitted disease**

ejaculation

The involuntary expelling of seminal fluid from the penis at the point of orgasm. A reflex action, it follows stimulation of the penis, such as masturbation or intercourse.

See also **ejaculatory incompetence**; **erection**; **orgasm**; **nocturnal emission**; **penis**; **premature ejaculation**; **retrograde ejaculation**; **semen**; **seminal fluid**

ejaculatory incompetence

A rare condition when a man is unable to ejaculate into a woman's vagina, even though there is no problem with other sorts of stimulus such as masturbation or fellatio; also called ***retarded ejaculation***. This can be brought on by trauma, religious or moral repression, homosexuality, dislike of a particular female partner or, in some cases, a simple fear of making a woman pregnant. Ironically a man with this problem can often maintain an erection during intercourse and keep his partner

orgasmic for long periods.
See also **ejaculation**; **orgasm**

embryo
The name given to the unborn child in its mother's womb from the fourth week after fertilization until the eighth week, when it becomes a foetus.
See also **foetus**; **pregnancy**; **XX and XY embryos**; **zygote**

endometriosis
A condition of unknown cause where the lining of the uterus (the endometrial tissue) becomes implanted in the ovaries or Fallopian tubes. It may cause infertility, but treatment by drug therapy or removal of cysts is available, and many women with this complaint can become pregnant.

endometritis
Inflammation of the lining of the uterus due to infection. Symptoms include lower abdominal pain, fever, and vaginal discharge. Causes include pelvic inflammatory disease, a complication of birth or abortion, the insertion of an intra-uterine device (IUD), or sexually transmitted disease. Treatment is by antibiotics and the removal of any foreign body (such as placental tissue or an IUD).
See also **intra-uterine device**; **uterus**

episiotomy /ɛpɪziːˈɒtəmi/
The surgical cutting of the tissue between the vagina and the anus at childbirth. Obstetricians disagree on the validity of episiotomy, some preferring the natural elasticity of the vagina to do its own job.

erection
The swelling, hardening, and upward-lifting of the penis at sexual stimulation, preparing it for penetration into the vagina. The penis becomes filled with blood, and the muscles around the blood vessels contract, preventing the blood from leaving

the penis until after ejaculation. Erections can occur during sleep and in very young boys for no apparent reason.

erogenous zones

Those parts of the body that are sexually sensitive, or cause sexual arousal when touched. They include the breasts, genitals, and mouth. The term derives from Greek *Eros*, originally in Homer as 'erotic desire', but in mythology, the god of love, the son of Aphrodite and Ares.

erotica

Sexually stimulating material. The term includes a vast (and to some extent unpredictable) range of stimulants, such as nude pictures of the opposite sex, films of other people making love, the feel of silk underwear, the first bite of a ripe plum, or the throbbing of a powerful motorbike.

eunuch

A male whose testicles have been removed, and who thus lacks male hormones. His features will be more feminine, such as a high-pitched voice, broad hips and narrow shoulders. In some countries, castrated young boys were employed to guard harems. The word derives from Greek *eune* 'bed' + *echein* 'keep', ie keeper of the bedchamber.
See also **testicles**

excitement phase

See **sexual response cycle**

exhibitionism

One of the allurement paraphilias, which manifests in a man showing his penis to a stranger in order to shock; colloquially known as *flashing*. The exhibitionist then goes on to enjoy masturbation, or sexual intercourse with his partner. The allurement paraphilics separate the 'naughty' act (exposure, in this instance) from the act of intercourse itself.
See also **indecent exposure**

extra-marital sex

Sex outside a marriage, ie being unfaithful to one's partner, committing adultery. The Kinsey Report (1990) suggests that 40% of married men and 20% of married women in America engage in extra-marital sex.

See also **adultery**

F

facts of life

Information about sexual reproduction, traditionally beginning with the birds and bees, then leading to human sexuality. Public opinion varies as to at what age children should be informed about sex. An enormous range of books is available, from picture books for the very young child, giving basic information about how babies are made (with the emphasis on mummy and daddy cuddling), to books for teenagers and adults, such as this one, which give information about all aspects of sexuality.

Fallopian tubes

The two tubes which are available to carry the egg and sperm from the uterus to the ovary for fertilization.
See **Appendix**

family planning

See **contraception**

fanny

1 In American English, a widely-used colloquial term for the male or female bottom. **2** In British English, a mildly taboo word for a woman's **genitalia**.

fellatio

See **oral sex**

female condom

See **condom**

fertility

The ability to produce children. Fertile men can produce healthy sperm in the testes, achieve an erection, and ejaculate semen into the vagina during sexual intercourse. Fertile woman

produce healthy ova (eggs), and their reproductive systems are capable of receiving sperm, and implanting and maintaining a fertilized egg through pregnancy.
See also **ejaculation**; **erection**; **intercourse, sexual**; **pregnancy**

fetishism
Sexual arousal which relies on the stimulation of particular objects (not necessarily sexual), such as leather or rubber clothing, high-heeled shoes, underwear, or even feet. Treatment is rare except in cases of criminality, such as stealing, and many fetishists find willing partners.
See also **frottage**; **paraphilia**

fetus
See **foetus**

fisting
The term used to describe inserting the hand or fist into the partner's rectum or vagina for sexual stimulation. A high-risk activity, it may cause numerous problems and can be fatal if pressure is inadvertently put on certain internal organs.

fixation
A Freudian term describing the attachment of sexual drive to an event, real or imagined, experienced in childhood. Freud suggests that children go through ***oral***, ***anal***, and ***phallic*** stages of development, and that these stages are connected with the child's early relationship with its mother. Fixations are unconscious; powerful ones can lead to regressive behaviour where the person is driven by childlike reactions, and are believed by many psychoanalysts to be the cause of some emotional disorders.
See also **Freud, Sigmund**

flaccid /'flæksɪd/
A term commonly used to describe the non-erect state of the penis.
See also **erection**; **penis**

flagellation
A type of fetish, in which sexual stimulation is derived from being beaten by, or from beating, one's partner.
See also **fetishism**; **paraphilia**; **sado-masochism**

flashing
See **exhibitionism**

flush
See **sex flush**

foetus *or* **fetus**
The term given to the unborn child from the eighth week of conception to birth. It develops in the uterus, cushioned by amniotic fluid, and nourished via the placenta, which is attached to the foetus by the umbilical cord.
See also **pregnancy**; **uterus**

foreplay
The activities engaged in between sexual partners to stimulate sexual intensity, before performing sexual intercourse. They include kissing and touching each other, including the genital areas. Sex therapists may encourage exploring your own body, learning how men's and women's bodies work, getting to know what gives you pleasure, being selfish as well as giving, taking time to find out what your partner likes, and discovering what you like to do together.
See also **intercourse, sexual**

foreskin
The sleeve of skin, which protects the tip of the penis; also known as the *prepuce*. By the time adulthood is reached the foreskin normally retracts fully when the penis is erect.
See also **circumcision**; **coronal ridge**; **foreskin, infections of**; **penis**

foreskin, infections of

Infections affecting the foreskin part of the penis. The most common include *phimosis*, where the foreskin is too tight to pull back or retract from the penis, and infection develops under the foreskin; this happens from the age of five, and can be avoided by attention to hygiene. *Balanitis* is an infection and inflammation of the head of the penis and foreskin, with painful erection; this may recur from puberty. *Paraphimosis* is a related disorder where the foreskin is stuck in the retracted position, and the **glans** swells painfully.
See also **Appendix**; **penis**

fornication

[Latin *fornicare* 'to arch, bend over'] Voluntary sexual intercourse between an unmarried man and an unmarried woman. In biblical terms it referred to adultery.

French kiss

A mouth to mouth kiss where one person inserts the tongue into another's mouth, or the tongues meet.

French letter

See **condom**

frenulum

The sensitive piece of skin on the underside of the penis where it meets the **glans**.
See also **Appendix**

Freud, Sigmund

(1856–1939)
The founder of psychoanalysis, born in Austria. He studied medicine, specializing in neurology and psychopathology. He believed in infantile sexuality, and was the first to identify the **Oedipus complex**. He argued also that dreams are disguised manifestations of repressed sexual desires, and named the three

stages of child development as the ***oral***, ***anal***, and ***phallic*** stages.
See also **fixation**

frigidity
The state of being averse to sexual contact. The term is commonly used in a somewhat mocking way by (usually) men when their partner is disinterested in the sexual act, but true frigidity occurs when a woman who is in a mutually loving relationship with a man, and who is not consciously frightened of sex, wants to have intercourse, but fails to enjoy it despite all efforts. This can be caused by the effect of drugs, pregnancy, childbirth, or psychological problems.

frottage /ˈfrɒtɑːʒ/ *or* **frotteurism**
The act of rubbing oneself against another for sexual stimulation; more specifically of a fully-clothed man rubbing his genital area against a woman's buttocks, for instance, on a crowded train. Such behaviour is indicative of an inability to form successful relationships with the opposite sex, and a possible fetish about buttocks.
See also **fetishism**; **paraphilia**

frotteurism
See **frottage**

fuck
See **intercourse, sexual**

G

gamete intra-fallopian transfer
See **GIFT**

gardnerella
A nonspecific vaginal infection. Symptoms are often absent, but there may be an unpleasant odour and a discharge. The recommendations for treatment vary, and may include antibiotics. Recurrence is common, with the likelihood of being reinfected by the male partner. The causes are unclear, but are believed to include: childbirth, having a cervical infection, having more than one sexual partner, or the use of an **intra-uterine device**.

gay
See **homosexual**

genitalia
The reproductive organs of the male and female. The term usually refers to the external or visible genital organs: the penis and the scrotum (which holds the testes), in the male; the vulva, clitoris, and vagina, in the female. The internal genitalia include the prostate gland, seminal vesicles, and vas deferens in the male, and the Fallopian tubes, uterus, and ovaries in the female.
See also **Appendix**; **pubic hair**

genophobia
Fear of sexual intercourse. The term derives from Greek *geno* 'offspring' + *phobos* 'fear'.

GIFT
The abbreviation of *gamete intra-fallopian transfer*, an infertility treatment for use in women who have normal Fallopian tubes. The ovaries are stimulated by drugs, then fluid is sucked out

from the ovarian follicles and examined for eggs. The eggs are replaced in the Fallopian tube, together with some semen. This procedure is carried out using an instrument known as a *laparoscope*, under a general anaesthetic.

gigolo /ˈdʒɪgəloʊ/
A kept man, used for sexual satisfaction, usually younger than the woman who keeps him. The word originally meant 'dancing partner', deriving from French *gigolette* 'woman who frequents public dances', and thus one of easy virtue.

ginseng
A thick-rooted perennial, native to N America and Asia. The root is said to have aphrodisiac qualities.
See also **aphrodisiac; mandrake**

glans
The head of the penis.
See also **Appendix; coronal ridge; frenulum; penis**

gonads
The sex glands, responsible for the production of reproductive cells within the **embryo**. If the cells carry a Y chromosome the gonads produce testicles; if not, they eventually grow into ovaries. The word is also used as slang for **testicles**.
See also **XX and XY embryos**

gonorrhoea /gɒnəˈriːə/
One of the oldest known *sexually transmitted diseases*, recorded from as far back as 400 BC; commonly called *clap*. Infection of the urinary tract in the male results in painful or difficult urination. Many women have no symptoms and the disease quietly causes damage to the reproductive organs, leading to pelvic inflammatory disease and infertility. Gonorrhoea may also be transmitted during birth from mother to baby. Treatment is by antibiotics.
See also **sexually transmitted disease**

gross indecency

An unlawful sexual act between a man and another adult or child. Gross indecency falls short of intercourse, but generally involves some sort of physical contact; for example, a man exposing himself to a stranger while masturbating, or touching the genitals of a boy in his care. In the UK, it is a prosecutable offence for a man to commit an act of gross indecency towards a child under 14, or with a male under the age of 21.

See also **frottage**; **homosexual**

group sex

Sexual intercourse taking place with more than two people involved on one occasion. A high-risk activity, it is estimated that less than 2 per cent of the Western population is ever involved in group sex, and then usually only once. Research has turned up very little about group sex. It seems that invitations are by word of mouth and that each 'group' makes its own rules as to what sort of sexual activities take place.

gynaecomastia /gaɪniːkəˈmæstiə/

The swelling or enlargement of the male breasts. Major causes include tumours, and cirrhosis of the liver. Excessive intake of alcohol almost invariably causes some swelling of the breasts (in males); and almost half of all adolescent boys experience temporary gynaecomastia. Any man who notices a change in the shape or appearance of his breasts should seek medical advice.

See also **breasts**

H

harassment (sexual)

A situation which typically involves a senior colleague making unwanted sexual advances either verbally or physically to a junior, thus placing the employee in the difficult position of putting their job at risk if the advances are rebuffed. It is generally encountered in the workplace, and is a criminal offence.

hermaphrodite

A person whose body contains both male and female reproductive organs. The term derives from *Hermaphroditus*, the son of Aphrodite and Hermes in Greek mythology, a god with **bisexual** characteristics. The nymph Salmacis, unloved by him, prayed to be united with him; this was granted by combining them in one body.
See also **pseudo-hermaphrodism**

herpes /ˈhɛ:pi:z/

A viral infection which affects the vulvo-vaginal region, mouth or lips. A rash is followed by the appearance of small blisters which may ulcerate and become infected. The virus lies dormant between recurrent attacks, which are common.

heterosexual

A person sexually attracted to members of the opposite sex. The term derives from the Greek *hetero* 'other, different', and contrasts with **homosexual**.
See also **homosexual; bisexual**

hirsutism

An excessive amount of hair on the body, usually in women. It occurs in many normal women, especially after the menopause, but it may be a symptom of disease, such as *polycystic ovary syndrome* and *congenital adrenal hyperplasia*.

HIV

See **AIDS**

homophobia

Fear or hatred of homosexuals. It is often based on the untrue but stereotyped beliefs that all homosexuals are child molesters or that they can corrupt young boys.

homosexual

Someone who chooses to have an intimate sexual and romantic relationship with a person or persons of the same sex. The term commonly refers to males; female homosexuals are usually called **lesbians**. Studies carried out by the Kinsey Institute in the 1940s indicate that in America approximately 4 per cent of adult males are exclusively homosexual, and up to one third have had a homosexual experience leading to orgasm at some time. In 1967 the Sexual Offences Act removed private homosexual liaison between consenting adults from criminal law; research has indicated that the more lenient attitude applied towards homosexuality since then has not increased the numbers of people having homosexual experiences. It is not known why some individuals develop homosexuality. The word *gay* is often used to mean homosexual.

See also **latent homosexual**; **lesbian**; **outing**

hormone replacement therapy (HRT)

The use of oestrogen hormones to treat the hormonal deficiency which causes symptoms accompanying the menopause. The symptoms include hot flushes and night sweats, thinning and dryness of the vagina, reduction in bone density, and narrowing of the arteries. The therapy is usually given in combination with progestogen to avoid the increase in susceptibility to cancer of the uterus. The drugs are given orally in a monthly cycle, and treatment continues for two to five years. Regular health checks are carried out during this period. Hormone replacement therapy is not advisable for women who have suffered from a stroke, thrombosis, liver disease, hypertension, cancer of the

breast or uterus, or who are heavy smokers.
See also **atrophic vaginitis**; **hot flush**; **menopause**

hot flush

A sensation, experienced by some menopausal women, of being too hot, accompanied by sweating, and reddening of the face, neck, and chest. In some cases, it can be treated by hormone replacement therapy.
See also **hormone replacement therapy**; **menopause**

HPV

See **human papillomavirus**

HRT

See **hormone replacement therapy**

human papillomavirus (HPV)

Genital warts. It is a ***sexually transmitted disease***, more common in men and women between 20 and 24 years of age, which can be treated and often eliminated. Cancer of the cervix is associated with HPV infection, and any man or woman having genital warts should avoid sexual contact until treated.

hydrocele /'haɪdroʊsiːl/

A condition whereby the space between the inner layer of the scrotum and the outer layer of the testicles becomes filled with fluid. It is a common condition in middle-age, and may be caused by inflammation, an infection or, more rarely, a tumour. Treatment is only necessary if there is pain or discomfort; the fluid is drawn off through a hollow needle under a local anaesthetic. A recurrence of the condition may require surgery.

hymen

The fine layer of tissue across the entrance to the vagina, present in young girls. The hymen can be torn as a result of sexual intercourse, inserting a tampon or fingers, or even as a result of sporting activity. Sometimes a slight spotting of blood occurs when the hymen is broken but it usually goes unnoticed. See also **vagina**; **virginity**

hypersexuality
An insatiable need for sex which interferes with everyday life. It rarely involves emotional involvement with one sexual partner. See also **nymphomania**; **satyriasis**

hysterectomy
Surgical removal of the uterus, performed to treat cancer, fibrous tumours, menorrhagia, endometriosis, or prolapsed uterus. It is one of the most common operations in the UK. In a total hysterectomy, the Fallopian tubes and ovaries are removed as well as the uterus and the cervix. After a hysterectomy a woman is infertile, and has no periods; she can resume sexual relations about a month later, or whenever comfortable. See also **Appendix**; **endometriosis**; **menorrhagia**; **uterus**

I

impotence

The inability in a male to achieve or maintain an erection in order to engage in sexual intercourse. A minority (10 per cent) of cases of impotence are caused by organic diseases: these include inadequate secretion of sex hormones by the pituitary gland or the testes; conditions such as diabetes, and other severe debilitating diseases. More commonly a number of psychological causes are responsible: these include attitudes to sex held by the man or his partner; marital, family, or social relationships; and the strength of the sexual drive. ***Secondary impotence*** is used to describe impotence which occurs temporarily in an otherwise sexually active person; ***primary impotence*** is diagnosed when a male has never been able to achieve an erection for the purposes of sexual intercourse. Treatment is available for impotence caused by a physical disorder (eg vasodilating drugs, **penile implants**), and **sex therapy** or counselling is successful in more than 50 per cent of long-term cases with psychological causes.

incest

Sexual intercourse between people who are so closely related that they are forbidden by law to marry. In English law, incest is an offence when intercourse takes place between a man and his daughter, grand-daughter, mother, sister, or half-sister; or between a woman of 16 or over and her father, brother, son, grandfather, or half-brother, even with her consent. In Scotland sexual intercourse between an aunt and a nephew, or an uncle and a niece is also an incest offence. Incest is punishable by up to 7 years in jail, or by life imprisonment if committed with a girl under the age of 13. It is not an offence if both parties are adult and are unaware that they are related; nor can a girl under 16 be prosecuted for incest.

incubus

An evil male spirit who seeks sexual intercourse with sleeping

women. The believed offspring of such a union are witches and demons. The existence of incubi was legally recognized in the Middle Ages.
See also **succubus**

indecent exposure

An offence of exposing the private parts of one's body. The typical case is of a man exposing his genitalia: this is an offence if at least two people could have seen the exposure, even if it has offended no-one. If a man exposes his genitalia to a woman in a violent or alarming way, he may be guilty of indecent assault.
See also **exhibitionism**

infantilism

One of the ***paraphilias*** in which sexual arousal or orgasm can be achieved only as a result of pleasures recalled from babyhood. These include the practice of wearing nappies or rubber pants, sleeping in a cot, and being fed from a bottle.
See also **paraphilia**

infertility

The inability of a male and female to produce children; also called ***sterility***. Approximately 10 per cent of couples experience some form of infertility, and there are many factors affecting it. Conception takes place only where the male produces healthy sperm, the woman produces healthy eggs, and through sexual intercourse the sperm reaches the woman's Fallopian tubes without obstruction. The sperm must then be capable of fertilizing the egg at the appropriate time, and the fertilized egg must be able to implant itself in the uterus. At that point conditions in the uterus must allow the healthy development of the embryo. Any irregularity in this chain of events may cause infertility. Problems encountered in the male include the absence or inadequate production of sperm, or of sperm with impaired mobility. In the female, ovulation may not take place, there may be infection present, there may be an obstruction in the Fallopian tubes, or physical abnormalities in the uterus. Treatments include hormone therapy, microsurgery to repair damaged Fallopian tubes, and several other techniques. (See also **gamete intra-fallopian transfer**; *in vitro* **fertilization**; **pregnancy**.)

infibulation
A form of circumcision of the female in which the outer lips of the vagina (the labia majora) are removed surgically, and the entrance to the vagina is made smaller, by stitching. This operation is ritually carried out without anaesthetic on young girls in parts of Africa. See also **circumcision, female**.

insemination, artificial
See **artificial insemination**

intercourse, sexual
In general, a form of sexual activity during which the man inserts his erect penis into a woman's vagina for the purpose of pleasure, leading to orgasm, or for the purpose of achieving fertilization. Loosely, it can mean a variety of sexual activities. A large number of slang terms are available to describe the activity: these include the highly taboo *fuck*, the moderately impolite *screw* and *shag*, and the mildly humorous *bonk*.
See also **missionary position**; **rape**; **sexual response cycle**

intra-uterine device (IUD)
A form of **contraception** comprising a spring-like device which is inserted through the vagina into the uterus by a medical practitioner; also known as a *coil* or *loop*. Made from moulded plastic, or with copper wire wound around the stem, most IUDs have a plastic string which hangs down from the cervix into the vagina, facilitating location at the time of removal. They do not prevent ovulation and are not spermicidal, but function by preventing the implantation of the fertilized egg into the wall of the uterus. IUDs are recommended for the mature women who has already had pregnancies. They are not suitable for women who suffer from pelvic infection, painful periods or fibroids (fibrous tumours).

IUD

See **intra-uterine device**

in vitro fertilization

The process of treating **infertility** by surgically removing an egg from the ovary and fertilizing it outside the body. This may be performed when there is absence of or damage to the Fallopian tubes, when the man's sperm count is low, or when sperm is unable to survive in the woman's cervical mucus. Although success rates are continuing to improve, it is an expensive and not altogether successful technique, with only 10-20 per cent culminating in a pregnancy. It is performed by first giving the woman drugs to stimulate ovulation; several ova are taken from the surface of the ovaries by a process known as ***laparoscopy*** and placed in a suitable medium to which spermatozoa are added. About 40 hours later the ova are examined to confirm that fertilization has occurred, after which the fertilized egg is transferred to the uterus via the vagina and cervix. In lay language, the phrase ***test-tube baby*** has widespread use.
See also **infertility**

J

Johnny

See **condom**

Johnson, Virginia (E Shelman)

(1925–)

American psychologist and sexologist, born in Springfield, Missouri. Educated at Missouri University, she joined with William Masters' group in 1957, and achieved fame through their investigations of the physiology of sexual intercourse.

See also **Masters, William**

K

Kama Sutra

The classic Hindu text on the pursuit of sensual and aesthetic love, attributed to the sage Vatsyayana. In mythology, ***Kama*** is the Hindu god of love, personifying the creative impulse; ***Sutra*** is a text or religious book of the Hindus. The Kama Sutra is remembered mainly in the West for its interesting variety of sexual positions, and there are now videos available of its teachings.

Kinsey, Alfred C(harles)

(1894–1956)

American sexologist and zoologist, born in Hoboken, New Jersey. He was professor of zoology at Indiana University from 1920, and in 1942 was the founder-director of a research institute there for the scientific study of human sexual behaviour, the first of its kind. He published two studies, ***Sexual Behaviour in the Human Male*** (1948, the so-called ***Kinsey Report***), and ***Sexual Behaviour in the Human Female*** (1953).

The Kinsey Institute for Research in Sex, Gender, and Reproduction was formed when the Association of Women Students at the University demanded a course in human sexuality. Kinsey was asked to coordinate the course, and his vision was to supply accurate data with which individuals and society could make informed decisions about sexual behaviour. The ***Kinsey Report*** started life as a newspaper column following the Institute's success in publishing data of this kind. The Institute continues to publish work in this area, notably the ***Kinsey Institute New Report on Sex*** (Penguin, 1990).

L

labia majora /ˈleɪbiə mæˈdʒɔːrə/

The external fleshy lips of the female **genitalia**, or vulva, which protect the vaginal opening. They are hairy, and contain sweat glands.
See also **vulva**

labia minora /ˈleɪbiə mɪˈnɔːrə/

The internal lips of the female **genitalia**, or vulva. They meet to form the hood of the clitoris, and are protected by the outer lips.
See also **vulva**

latent homosexual

Generally, a male with homosexual tendencies which are hidden. It has come particularly to mean a male with suppressed or disowned homosexual tendencies. (See also **homosexual**.)

lesbian

Female homosexuality; the sexual attraction and expression of passion between women. It is often politically linked with feminism. The word comes from the Greek island of Lesbos where legend has it that the population was entirely female, and any male intruders were put to death. The poetess Sappho (c.600 BC), who lived on ***Lesbos***, was accused of unnatural relations with other women.

libido

See **lust**

loop

See **intra-uterine device**

love bite

A small bruise on the skin inflicted by sucking it against the teeth during sexual excitement. The most popular places for love bites are on women's breasts, and on the necks of teenagers of both sexes. Other sites include the shoulder, bottom, and palm of the hand. It is considered dangerous to inflict love bites on or close to the genitals.

love-making

The physical expression of love between partners, especially as manifested in sexual intercourse. One of the most natural human acts, it can be fraught with tension and anxieties, and no matter how instinctive it is, there are techniques which have to be learned if the act of sexual intercourse is to achieve a profound level of love-making. One of the oldest sources of learning these skills is the ***Kama Sutra***, and many young men's and women's magazines run illuminating and comprehensive articles on the subject.
See also **intercourse, sexual**; **Kama Sutra**

lover's balls

A colloquial description of the temporary ache or discomfort in the testicles which some men experience on sexual arousal without ejaculation or intercourse; also called ***blue balls***. It also affects the **vulva** of some women, and the sensation is caused by congestion of blood in the genital area. It is relieved either by masturbation, sexual activity or removal of the stimulus. No permanent physical harm seems to arise from this discomfort.

lubricant

In the context of sexuality, a water-based substance to lubricate the vagina during sexual intercourse. Lubricants are available without prescription, and are useful for comfortable **penetration** when the woman's vagina is rather dry. It should be noted that oil-based or petroleum-based products such as Vaseline® or Nivea® should NOT be used as sexual lubricants. Only water-soluble creams and jellies (such as K-Y Jelly®) are non-

allergic and do not quickly weaken or make holes in condoms, diaphragms, etc.
See also **spermicide**

lust
Strong sexual desire or appetite, often distinguished from ***love***; technically (in psychology) referred to as ***libido*** /lɪbi:doʊ/. In religious contexts, lust is viewed as the sinful and sinister desire for (probably illicit) sexual pleasures.

M

making love
See **love-making**

mammary glands
See **breasts**

mandrake
A supposed aphrodisiac. It is a plant of the potato family, native to the Mediterranean area, whose large forked root was thought to resemble the human form. It is considered to be the European version of ginseng.
See also **aphrodisiac**

masochism
Sexual activity in which there is a desire to have pain inflicted on oneself. Considered to be a psychosexual disorder, the term derives from Austrian author Leopold von Sacher-Masoch (1836–95), who wrote extensively on his own pleasure in being beaten. The masochist generally has some control over the situation in which he/she is humiliated or whipped, and will commonly seek a partner with whom he/she can indulge in sado-masochism.
See also **paraphilia**, **sadism**

Masters, William H(owell)
(1915–)
American gynaecologist and sexologist, born in Cleveland, Ohio. Educated at Rochester University, he joined the faculty of the Washington University School of Medicine (St Louis) in 1947. His studies in the psychology and physiology of sexual intercourse were carried out using volunteer subjects under laboratory conditions at the Reproductive Biology Research Foundation. Much of his research was done in collaboration with Virginia Johnson, whom he married in 1971 (divorced in

1992), and with whom he published *Human Sexual Response* (1966), which became an international best-seller. They also wrote *On Sex and Human Loving* (1986), and several other books. See also **Johnson, Virginia**

masturbation
The manual stimulation of the genitals for sexual pleasure, usually to **orgasm**. Now widely accepted as normal behaviour, in the 19th century it was believed to cause insanity, blindness and other disorders, probably because people suffering from forms of brain damage were sometimes seen to masturbate in public. Masturbating in public may be a sign of mental illness, but masturbation in private is certainly not a cause of it. Methods used in the 19th century in America to discourage childhood masturbation included applying leeches or an electric current to the genitals, castration, and clitorectomy, There are hundreds of slang terms for the activity, including *crank*, *flog the log*, *jack off*, *jerk off*, *toss off*, and *wank*.
See also **onanism**; **self abuse**

matrimonial position
See **missionary position**

ménage à trois /məˈnɑːz ɑː ˈtrwɑː/
[French, 'household of three'] A situation of a married couple living in the same house with the lover of one of the couple; more generally, sexual activity between three in a bed. It appears that both of these behaviours are rare in practice, though they crop up somewhat more often in fantasies.

menarche /ˈmɛnɑːkiː/
The first menstrual period in life; the first periodic discharge of blood from the vagina of females at the onset of puberty. It usually occurs around the age of 13, and is a significant event for which girls should be prepared, both physically and mentally. In some Asian and African cultures, the menarche is ritually celebrated by the entire family.
See also **menstruation**

menopause

The natural cessation of menstruation (and fertility) which occurs uniquely in human females around the age of 45–50 years; also called the ***change of life***. Its symptoms include sweating, hot flushes, vaginitis, depression, insomnia, and fatigue. The term comes from Greek ***men*** 'month', and originally referred to the end of the monthly cycle.
See also **climacteric**; **hormone replacement therapy**

menorrhagia /mɛnəˈreɪdʒɪə/

Excessive menstrual bleeding of more than three ounces. It commonly arises from disorders of the hormonal system or abnormalities of the uterus such as polyps or tumours.

menstruation

A discharge from the vagina of blood, mucus, and debris from the mucous membrane of the uterus, in response to hormonal changes. This occurs at approximately 28-day intervals in women of child-bearing age, except during pregnancy.
See also **pre-menstrual tension**; **sanitary towel**; **tampon**

mini pill

The progestogen-only **contraceptive pill** (oestrogen-free) which is taken daily without a break. Unlike other oral **contraceptives** which affect the hormonal system, the mini pill is effective as a contraceptive by thickening the cervical secretions and Fallopian tubes, preventing the sperm from reaching the egg. Although it has a higher failure rate than the oestrogen/progestogen pill, it is safer for women over 35, but it may cause irregular bleeding, and women using it must have annual gynaecological checks.
See also **contraceptive pill**

miscarriage

The spontaneous abortion or expulsion of the foetus before it is capable of life outside the womb. The most likely time for miscarriage to occur is within the first twelve weeks of pregnancy.
See also **abortion**

missionary position

Popularly believed to be the most common position for sexual intercourse, with the woman lying on her back and the man on top of her, face to face; also called the *matrimonial position*. The origins of the term are unclear, but various stories suggest that missionaries to Third World countries 'did it' that way and the tribesmen and women they preached to found it odd, because they did it woman-on-top.
See also **intercourse, sexual**

monogamy

The practice of having only one marriage partner at a time, as opposed to bigamy (having two) or polygamy (having more than two). Bigamy and polygamy are prosecutable offences in the UK.
See also **bigamy**; **polygamy**

monorchism

The complete absence of one of the two male testes. It is usually a congenital problem, except where one testis has been removed surgically. This condition is not to be confused with a testis which has not descended into the scrotum (*cryptorchidism*).
See also **testicles**

mons

The fatty area forming a slight mound over the pubic bone of the adult female, and covered with pubic hair. It is also known as the *mound of Venus* (the Roman goddess of love), from Latin *mons veneris*.

morning-after pill

A post-coital contraceptive pill used for emergency situations such as following **rape**. Containing the synthetic oestrogen stilbestrol, it prevents implantation of any fertilized egg. It is not safe for routine use.
See also **contraceptive pill**

mound of Venus
See **mons**

muco-thermal contraception
See **rhythm method**

N

necrophilia

Possibly the most extreme and perverse **paraphilia**, the desire to have sexual intercourse with a dead person. The term also includes any erotic interest in or obsession with corpses.

nipple

The projection on a woman's breast, usually pink or brownish in colour, where the mammary gland terminates, and from which a baby can suckle milk. It is one of the **erogenous zones**, which may be stroked or sucked during sexual **foreplay**. In males, the nipple is immature and without function, although for some men its stimulation gives sensual pleasure.
See also **areola**

nocturnal emission

Ejaculation of semen while asleep. This is a fairly normal occurrence for a sexually aware adolescent boy and is usually the result of a sexual dream (or *wet dream*). Orgasm in sleep only occurs in humans; some females do experience it when they are fully adult, but much more rarely than the male.

non-coital sex

Any kind of sexual activity which does not involve the penetration of the penis into the vagina.
See also **coitus**; **foreplay**

nymphomania

[Greek *nymphe* 'bride' + *mania* 'frenzy'] The condition describing a woman who has an uncontrollable and unusually high sex drive, and who rarely achieves physical or emotional satisfaction, even through orgasm or multiple relationships. It is commonly misused in the description of women who have numerous sexual partners.
See also **satyriasis**

O

Oedipus complex /ˈiːdɪpəs/

A term coined by Freud, and used in psychoanalysis, to refer to the erotic feelings of a son for his mother (at any age), and a sense of competitiveness towards the father. It derives from the Greek legend of *Oedipus*, a Theban hero who was foretold he would kill his father for his mother's hand in marriage. He left his adoptive parents, killed his natural father unwittingly, and married (again unwittingly) his real mother. When the truth was revealed to him he blinded himself. Nowadays sexual therapy or counselling would be made available to him.

See also **Freud, Sigmund**

onanism

Masturbation. The term comes from the biblical story of *Onan* (Genesis 38. 9–11), who '. . . spilled his seed on the ground so as not to raise up offspring . . .'. The story is now generally thought to be referring to **coitus interruptus**, but onanism is, however mistakenly, still used to refer to **masturbation**.

oral sex

Stimulation of the partner's genitals by mouth or tongue. Stimulation of the female genitals in this way is called *cunnilingus* /kʌnɪˈlɪŋgəs/ (slang: *muff-diving*), from Latin *cunnus* 'vulva' + *lingere* 'lick'. Stimulation of the male genitals is called *fellatio* /fəˈleɪʃəʊ/ (slang: *blow job*), from Latin *fellare* 'suck'. Oral sex is practised quite commonly as foreplay to increase arousal or to bring the partner to orgasm. However, a few states in the USA still regard oral-genital sex as a form of **sodomy** and hold it to be illegal.

orgasm

The sudden, intensely pleasurable rhythmic muscular contractions experienced by males and females at the height of sexual arousal. There is an abrupt increase in pulse rate and blood

pressure. In females, orgasm consists of between three and ten contractions (less than one second apart) of the vagina and the uterus. In males, ejaculation is inevitable at orgasm when similar contractions of the penis and urethra force semen out of the tip of the penis. The intensity and sensation of orgasm differs from person to person and can range from a slight throb to involuntary thrashing of the whole body. To *come* is a common description for reaching orgasm.
See also **orgasm, multiple**; **orgasm, mutual or simultaneous**; **sexual response cycle**

orgasm, multiple

The experience (usually a woman's) of having several orgasms during one period of sexual stimulation or intercourse. Kinsey reports that 8–9 per cent of women questioned in the 1940s and 1950s reported achieving multiple orgasms; and of these the majority had no more than two or three orgasms.
See also **Kinsey, Alfred C(harles)**; **orgasm**

orgasm, mutual *or* simultaneous

A situation when a man and a woman reach a sexual *climax* at the same moment, during vaginal intercourse; otherwise known as 'coming together'. Studies have shown that it is quite uncommon, and does not necessarily enhance a couple's sex-life; for many people, bringing a partner to orgasm independently is one of the greatest pleasures.
See also **orgasm**

orgasmic dysfunction

The inability of a woman to experience orgasm. The term *primary orgasmic dysfunction* (often nowadays called *anorgasmia*) refers to never having had an orgasm; *secondary orgasmic dysfunction* refers to having had an orgasm or orgasms at some point, but subsequently being unable to. There are many physical and psychological factors involved, including simply not being 'turned on' by one's partner, not being able to achieve orgasm by intercourse alone, or fear of sexual stimulation or intercourse. Most women can be successfully treated for an

orgasmic dysfunction by counselling and masturbation therapy.
See also **orgasm**

orgasmic phase

See **sexual response cycle**

outing

Originally in American English, now more generally, a man's public acceptance of himself as a practising homosexual. The term is also increasingly used with reference to women.
See also **homosexual**

ovary

The female organ of reproduction, in which the eggs or ova are produced. The production of the ova (eggs), and their release from the ovaries, ready for fertilization, is called ***ovulation***.
See also **pregnancy**

ovulation

See **ovary**

P

paederasty

See **pederasty**

paedophilia or pedophilia

The desire to have sexual intercourse with a partner who is a child, or pre-pubescent. In its mildest form, only fondling of a child takes place, but at its worst, groups of paedophiles (paedophile rings) abduct children, sexually abuse, and murder them. Most paedophiles are men who have personality problems and are unable to find satisfaction in normal relationships; it is extremely rare in women. In Western countries paedophilia is generally regarded as the most serious sexual offence; severe penalties are inflicted particularly on males who sexually abuse young boys. At least half of men charged with paedophilia are related to or acquainted with the child in question. Because of an increased awareness (or frequency) of child abuse, the British government announced changes (1993) in the way staff are selected for children's homes, to prevent paedophiles from gaining access to youngsters through child care work.

See also **sexual abuse**

Pap test

See **cervical smear**

paraphilia

[Greek *para* 'outside, beyond', + *philia* 'love'] A sexual *deviation* or *perversion*. The term covers a wide range of behaviour, from the slightly 'kinky' (eg the desire to be held down during intercourse), to the psychologically and physically harmful (eg sexual murder and rape).

paraphimosis

See **foreskin, infections of**

pederasty *or* **paederasty**
[Greek *paidos* 'boy' + *erastes* 'lover'] Anal intercourse with a boy. A man who acts this way is a *pederast*.
See also **paedophilia; sodomy**

pedophilia
See **paedophilia**

peeping Tom
See **voyeur**

pelvic inflammatory disease (PID)
A bacterial infection of the female internal organs (Fallopian tubes, uterus, and ovaries) which can cause infertility, or ectopic pregnancy. It is caused by some of the sexually transmitted diseases, infection through douching, the use of an intra-uterine device, or bacteria from the anus being transferred to the vagina. Symptoms are not always present, but can include lower abdominal pain, tenderness, and discharge or bleeding between menstrual periods. Treatment is available either by antibiotics or the surgical removal of the infected area.
See also **ectopic pregnancy; infertility**

penetration
Insertion of the man's erect penis into the woman's vagina in sexual intercourse.
See **intercourse, sexual**

penile glans
See **glans**

penile implant
An implant used in the penis to help men who, for medical reasons, cannot achieve erection, and for whom other treatment has been unsuccessful. There are two types in use. A *semi-rigid*

implant gives a man a permanent erection (which has to be pushed down by hand into the pants to conceal it), and is achieved by the surgical insertion of silicone. An **inflatable** system allows a man to achieve an erection when he desires, but a lengthy and complicated operation is required to insert silicone cylinders into the penis along with a pumping system operated by a manual valve on a tiny pump in the scrotum. Complications can arise with both systems, and may involve pain, shortening of the penis, lessening of sensitivity, and limited choice of sexual positions. These operations were first introduced in the 1970s, and thousands of penile implants have since been used with some success.
See also **penis**

penile ring
A rubber device placed around the base of the penis to stimulate blood flow into the penis in the hope of getting or maintaining an erection. The use of such aids is discouraged by the medical profession as they can lead to damage of the outer penis or the urethra, as well as infection.
See also **penis**

penis
The major part of the male external genitalia; less commonly known as the ***phallus***. It has a fixed root and a mobile body, covered with thin, elastic skin, and contains the urethra. The head (or glans) is largely covered by the **foreskin**, which in certain circumstances may be surgically removed. At rest the penis is in a **flaccid** state, but it becomes erect as a consequence of sexual stimuli. At the climax of sexual excitement, ejaculation of semen occurs, the penis then returning to its flaccid state. It is suggested that small flaccid penises lengthen by a greater amount than do large flaccid penises. Sexual difficulties rarely occur due to penis size if the erect penis is more than 2″ long. The average length of the erect penis (according to the 1990 Kinsey Report) is 5″ to 7″ long. The longest erect penis ever recorded was 13″, documented this century by Dr Robert L Dickinson, but the present author has failed to find any information on the

smallest. An enormous number of slang terms exist for **penis**, including ***cock***, ***prick***, ***dick***, ***knob***, ***willy***, and ***john***.
See also **erection**; **foreskin**; **penile implant**; **penile ring**; **phallic symbol**; **vasectomy**

periods
See **menstruation**

perversion
See **paraphilia**

petting
Sexual play. The term usually refers to that enthusiastic pre-sex fondling between heterosexual adolescents which, due to social, religious, or family restrictions, does not usually result in **penetration**.

phallic symbol
Anything vaguely penis-shaped and indicative of sexual power or the generative power of nature. Examples include cigarettes, chocolate bars, and lollipops, which are sometimes advertised being held suggestively in the mouth. In Victorian times, the maypole was bedecked with ribbons, and danced around by young girls during spring celebrations; and any tower, from high-rise buildings to the totem pole could be described as phallic.
See also **penis**

phallus
See **penis**

pheromones
Chemicals located in the apocrine glands under the arms and around the genitals in both sexes, whose aroma plays an important role in sexual signalling.
See also **cassolette**

phimosis
See **foreskin, infections of**

PID
See **pelvic inflammatory disease**

Pill, the
Any of various **contraceptive pills.**

pimp
One who procures; usually a man who engages or employs prostitutes, and supplies them with clients. The term is of unknown origin. (See also **procuration**; **prostitute**.)

plateau phase
See **sexual response cycle**

PMS (premenstrual syndrome)
See **premenstrual tension**

PMT
See **premenstrual tension**

polygamy
[Greek *polus* 'many' + *gamos* 'marriage'] Having more than one wife (or, less usually, husband) at the same time. This state is widely practised in some non-European countries, including many parts of Central Africa.
See also **bigamy**; **monogamy**.

pornography
Obscene literature. It is a term which has changed its meaning over the years. In the *Shorter Oxford Dictionary* (1933), it is defined as a 'description of the life, manners, etc. of prostitutes and their patrons . . .'. In the 1990 *Kinsey Report*, it is defined

more generally as 'erotica, sexually explicit material'. Pornography is one of the world's major industries, being the subject of many films, videos, and publications. Sometimes distinguished as either 'soft' or 'hard core', it generally represents the woman's body and sexuality in a demeaning and sometimes violent manner. Opinion varies as to whether pornographic material encourages men to become sexually violent towards women.

postillionage
Putting a finger in the partner's anus immediately prior to orgasm. The term is used widely in erotic French publications. It derives from the French ***postillon***, the rider of one of the horses harnessed to pull a carriage.

pregnancy
The period between conception (the implantation of a fertilized egg) and birth. Pregnancy in humans lasts approximately 40 weeks from the first day of the last menstrual period. Menstruation ceases for the duration; the uterus enlarges, and the breasts increase in size in preparation for lactation. At the first sign of pregnancy (usually a missed period), women are advised to seek antenatal care, and must avoid alcohol, drugs, and tobacco in order to prevent serious risk to the developing baby.
See also **ectopic pregnancy**; **embryo**; **fertility**; **foetus**; **infertility**; **pregnancy test**; **sterilization**

pregnancy, sex during
The practice of sexual intercourse during pregnancy. This is not thought to harm mother or baby when the pregnancy is normal and the mother desires it. However, if complications arise, such as pain, vaginal bleeding, or heavy secretions, intercourse should be stopped until a doctor is consulted. It can be fatal for the baby or cause defects if a pregnant woman has sexual intercourse with a partner carrying a sexually transmitted disease.
See also **intercourse, sexual**; **pregnancy**; **sexually transmitted disease**

pregnancy test

A test, performed either with a home-testing kit or by a doctor, usually at least ten days after a missed period. Pregnancy tests work by measuring the presence in the urine or blood of a hormone which is secreted only during pregnancy. A home-testing kit is used by mixing an early-morning urine sample with the test solution. The indicator stick supplied changes colour if there is a pregnancy.

premature ejaculation

Ejaculation before **penetration**, or soon enough afterwards for sex to be unsatisfying for one or both partners. The most common sexual problem for males, it is also the most responsive to treatment with sexual counselling.

See also **ejaculation**

premenstrual tension (PMT)

Emotional or physical symptoms experienced by women exclusively in the week or two before a period starts, and from which they find relief as soon as the menstrual flow begins; also called *premenstrual syndrome (PMS)*. Symptoms vary in nature and intensity and may include fatigue, depression, irrationality, irritability, headaches, tenderness of the breasts, crying, insomnia, fluid retention, and sinus trouble. Related to hormonal changes, the symptoms can sometimes be alleviated by use of the contraceptive pill, diuretic pills (which increase urine flow), low salt intake, and regular exercise.

See also **menstruation**

prepuce

See **foreskin**

priapism

The painful condition of a persistently erect penis, in the absence of sexual stimulation. It is indicative of the inability of the blood to flow away from the spongy tissue, and requires emergency medical treatment before permanent damage is done to the penis. The term derives from *Priapus*, a Greek god of fertility whose symbol was an erect phallus. Sometimes reported to be the son of Aphrodite and Dionysus, he was often represented as being the phallus itself, and rather bold statues of him guarded Greek and Roman gardens from c.330 BC.

prick-teaser
See **coquette**

primary impotence
See **impotence**

primary orgasmic dysfunction
See **orgasmic dysfunction**

procuration
The act of finding and supplying unlawful sexual partners for someone. The term usually refers to taking payment (commission) for sexual favours offered by a prostitute or homosexual. (See also **pimp**.)

promiscuous
[Latin *pro* 'forth' + *miscere* 'mixed'] A term which describes anyone who has sexual relationships with several partners, perhaps indiscriminately, or with more than is normally expected, given the social circumstances.

prophylactic
See **condom**

prostate gland
The gland surrounding the urethra which produces an alkaline fluid to help protect the sperms on the journey to the womb. It is believed by some doctors that regular emptying of the prostate gland (by ejaculation through intercourse or masturbation) decreases the chance of prostate problems. One in 11 American

men develop prostate cancer, and 50 per cent of of those over 50 suffer BPH (non-cancerous enlargement of the prostate). Medical advice should be sought if there are symptoms such as painful urination, blood in the urine, changes in the flow of urine, or back pain. (See also **sperm**; **urethra**.)

prostitute

A person (usually female) who offers herself (himself) for unlawful, paid, and often indiscriminate sexual intercourse; also called a ***whore***. Whoring was an acceptable trade until the 18th century, and the word was in common use, appearing frequently in the works of Shakespeare. From then on it became something of a taboo until the middle of the 20th century. Several modern names are now available, such as ***call girl*** and ***hooker***.

See also **pimp**; **tart**; **venal pleasures**

protective

See **condom**

pseudo-hermaphrodism

A hormonal disorder similar to true hermaphrodism, but in which a male has a male reproductive system whose outside genitalia appear female, or a woman has a female system, whose outside genitalia appear male.

See also **hermaphrodite**

puberty

The age when it is biologically possible to be capable of producing offspring. It generally refers to those years of development in which physical, psychological, and social changes take place in a child developing into physical adulthood. Puberty can begin as early as the age of 8, or as late as 15, and the process may take from 2 to 6 years.

See also **adolescence**

pubic hair

The short, coarse, curly hair that grows close to the genitalia on men and women. It first appears as fine down from some time after the age of nine, developing by the age of 18 in boys to cover the base of the penis, spreading upward towards the stomach and downwards towards the thighs, and by 19 in girls to form a triangular shape covering the fatty mound (***mons***) over the pubic bone, and over the outside of the outer lips of the vagina. There is no known biological function of the pubic hair. Some women experience a thinning of the hair during the menopause. See also **genitalia**

pubic lice

Also known as ***crabs***, an infestation of ***body lice*** in the pubic hair region. The lice are transmitted by direct contact with someone else carrying them. They lay eggs (***nits***) on hair and clothing, and may carry diseases such as typhus.

R

rape

The act of having sexual intercourse with a woman against her will, or without her conscious permission. In criminal law this includes instances where her permission has been extracted by force or fear of immediate bodily harm. Rape is punishable with life imprisonment. A man can be convicted of raping his wife, and research shows that most rapes are committed by husbands against their wives. Proof of rape includes full intercourse with the emission of semen, therefore women cannot be convicted of rape. However, a man can be raped by a women. In the very few cases reported, men have been able to have intercourse under the threat of physical violence, and have suffered similar psychological consequences to those of women who have been raped. The offence of rape by a man upon another man, or on a man by a woman is dealt with as a case of indecent assault.
See also **intercourse, sexual**

rear entry

A position of sexual intercourse where the man enters the woman from behind, either kneeling, standing, lying, or sitting; also referred to as the ***spoon*** position. It is believed by some to be the best position for fertilization, as the sperm is deposited near the cervix.
See also **intercourse, sexual**

rectal intercourse

See **anal intercourse**

resolution phase

See **sexual response cycle**

retarded ejaculation

See **ejaculatory incompetence**

retrograde ejaculation

Ejaculation where the semen goes back into the bladder rather than out through the urethra and out of the penis. This may be caused by diabetes, or surgery of the neck of the bladder, and is not usually correctable. However, the normal sensations of orgasm are rarely lost in this condition.
See also **ejaculation**

rhythm method

The 'natural' method of family planning without drugs or devices, whereby a couple do not have sexual intercourse during the woman's fertile time. At its simplest this means no intercourse for ten consecutive days in the middle of the menstrual cycle. The rhythm method has a high failure rate even with careful planning, which needs to take into account the dates of the menstrual flow, body temperature, and cervical mucus changes. When these techniques are used, the approach is also referred to as the *muco-thermal* method.
See also **contraception**; **safe period**

rimming

Placing the tongue into someone's anus for sexual stimulation. This practice is considered a high-risk sexual behaviour.

rubber

See **condom**

S

sadism

Sexual activity in which there is a desire to inflict pain on another. The word was provided by the name of the Marquis de *Sade* (1740-1814), a French writer who was condemned to death in 1772 for his sexual practices. He escaped but was later imprisoned, and while in jail wrote ***The 120 Days of Sodom***. At the time of his death he was insane.
See also **paraphilia**; **sado-masochism**

sado-masochism

Indulgence in sexual activites where to obtain arousal it is necessary for one partner to be hurt (**masochism**) and the other to do the hurting (**sadism**). The activities vary from spanking to the more serious inflicting of pain.
See also **masochism**; **paraphilia**; **sadism**

safe period

The time during the woman's monthly menstrual cycle when she is unlikely to be fertile.
See also **rhythm method**

safe sex

1 Sexual intercourse which is free from the possibility of pregnancy. **2** Sexual intercourse which avoids the possibility of contracting the AIDS virus or other sexually transmitted disease. The safest sex is a permanent mutually exclusive **heterosexual** relationship. The term now generally refers to the use of condoms. The Health Education Authority also suggests limiting the number of sexual partners, and avoiding risky practices.

saltpetre

Potassium nitrate (KNO_3) used in making gunpowder and as an agricultural fertilizer. It is reputed to be given orally to prisoners or others to reduce sexual desire, but its effect has never been scientifically proved.

sanitary towel

A disposable, absorbent pad used to catch the monthly menstrual flow of blood. Available in many different thicknesses and sizes, it may be attached to the gusset of pants by a sticky strip, or worn attached to an elastic ***sanitary belt*** by means of loops.

See also **menstruation**; **tampons**

satyriasis /sætəˈraɪəsɪs/

Male nymphomania, or a pathological sexual drive, often associated with psychiatric disorders. In extreme cases, individuals may be treated with female hormones, but the usual treatment is behavioural therapy and/or psychoanalysis. ***Satyrs*** were the spirits of wild life in Greek religion, the brothers of the Nymphs, often depicted as lewd and bestial. Later tradition associated them with the god Pan and with licence, and they became the symbols of male sexuality.

scabies /ˈskeɪbi:z/

[Latin ***scabere*** 'to scratch'] A contagious disease that can be passed on sexually or by sleeping in the same bed as someone infected. Itch mites burrow in the human skin and lay eggs. Symptoms are caused by an allergy to the mites and can take weeks to develop. It is treatable with a lotion which is applied to the entire body.

screw

See **intercourse, sexual**

scrotum

The wrinkled bag or pouch of skin which contains and protects the testicles from temperature variations. The scrotum shrivels up in order to conserve heat, and the wrinkles open out

immediately if the temperature rises too high. It is an important **erogenous zone** in men.
See also **cremasteric reflex**; **testicles**

secondary impotence
See **impotence**

secondary orgasmic dysfunction
See **orgasmic dysfunction**

self-abuse
The old-fashioned label for masturbation or solitary sexual indulgence. The term is nowadays more likely to be connected with the physical abusing of oneself (eg with a lighted cigarette) or, more commonly, with over-indulgence in alcohol or drugs.
See also **masturbation**

semen
The mixture of fluids and sperm ejaculated from the penis at the point of orgasm.
See also **ejaculation**; **seminal fluid**; **seminal vesicles**; **sperm**

seminal fluid
The liquid ejaculated from the penis at the point of orgasm, which carries sperms from the testicles. Each ejaculation of the seminal fluid contains up to 500 million sperms plus secretions from the prostate gland and seminal vesicles which help to nourish the sperms on their journey towards possible fertilization in the woman's womb.
See also **prostate gland**; **semen**; **seminal vesicles**

seminal vesicles
Small sacs connected to the urethra which produce nutrients for the sperms and incorporate an alkaline fluid to protect them from the acidity encountered when they reach the vagina.
See also **seminal fluid**

sex flush

A rash which may appear on the neck and chest of a woman at the height of sexual arousal. It disappears as the body returns to its non-aroused state.

sex therapy

A form of psychotherapy, or behaviour modification, for couples with sexual problems which stem from psychological factors. Couples are counselled and encouraged to talk through their problems, then simple remedial tasks can be given for them to practise within the privacy of their own home while they are undergoing counselling. Several weeks of counselling are usually offered. This form of treatment is used for non-medical problems such as **premature ejaculation**, lack of desire, **secondary impotence**, and **retarded ejaculation**.

sexual identity

The feeling or awareness of one's gender, as intrinsically male or female, and of how others see one. This sense of identity can become confused in the case of transsexuals or hermaphrodites.

sexual intercourse

See **intercourse, sexual**

sexual response cycle

The four phases of response in men and women during sexual intercourse: the *excitement phase*, the *plateau phase*, the *orgasmic phase*, and the *resolution phase*. This cycle was first reported by Masters and Johnson in *Human Sexual Response* (1966). The *excitement phase* is initiated by whatever is sexually stimulating for a particular individual. If effective, this leads to a state of increased tension (the *plateau phase*). The *orgasmic phase* is the involuntary response when the body changes reach their maximum intensity. The *resolution phase* is the lessening of tension as the individual returns to an unstimulated state.
See also **intercourse, sexual**; **Masters, William H(owell)**

sexually transmitted disease (STD)

An infection or illness caught from a sexual partner which may be transmitted to offspring before birth. Known until recently as *venereal disease*, there are more than 50 STDs, ranging from mild infections through those causing infertility and death. All are treatable and most are curable if treated early enough.
See also **AIDS**; **candida**; **chlamydia**; **gardnerella**; **gonorrhoea**; **herpes**; **pubic lice**; **scabies**; **syphilis**; **trichomoniasis**

shag

See **intercourse, sexual**

sheath

See **condom**

smear

See **cervical smear**

smegma

An unpleasant cheese-like material which can accumulate under the foreskin of the penis. The presence of smegma can be very unappetizing for a sexual partner, and a build-up of it may lead to inflammation of the penis, and the need for circumcision. This is prevented by retracting the foreskin and washing daily with soap and water. Doctors recommend teaching this routine to boys from about the age of five.
See also **penis**

sodomy

Copulation between males, or sexual relations between human and animal. The term derives from ***Sodom***, the name of the early city by the Dead Sea recorded in the Bible, and known as a wicked or corrupt place.
See also **anal intercourse**; **bestiality**; **buggery**

soixante-neuf /ˈswæzɒnt ˈnɜːf/

[French, '69'] A phrase used to graphically describe the sexual

position where mutual oral-genital stimulation can be carried out simultaneously between partners.
See also **oral sex**

Spanish Fly
See **cantharides**

sperm
The generative substance formed by a man which, when combined with a female egg inside the uterus, has the potential to develop into a foetus. Millions upon millions of sperms are produced in the male testicles, and during sexual intercourse up to 500 million can be ejaculated into the woman's vagina, ready to swim up to the uterus.
See also **semen**

spermicide
A chemical barrier substance that kills sperm, used to prevent pregnancy. Spermicides are generally available from pharmacies in the form of creams, and can be used with condoms and diaphragms for safer birth control. Oil- or petroleum-based lubricants destroy condoms and diaphragms, and should *never* be used as substitutes for spermicides.
See also **barrier method of contraception**; **condom**; **diaphragm**

squeeze technique
A form of therapy to delay male ejaculation. This involves the partner briefly squeezing the penis on the top and bottom surfaces, firstly at the coronal ridge near the head of the penis and, when the man has regained some control, at the base of the penis during penetration. Therapeutic tasks are best performed when backed up with counselling.
See also **sex therapy**

STD
See **sexually transmitted disease**

sterility

See **infertility**

sterilization

A surgical operation performed to permanently prevent conception. Male sterilization is performed by a minor operation called **vasectomy**. Female sterilization is more complicated, and a general anaesthetic is required. It involves opening the abdomen and cutting through the two Fallopian tubes. This means that the eggs released by the ovaries disappear harmlessly inside the abdomen, and the male sperms can no longer reach them. ***Laparascopic*** sterilization is a technique which does not involve cutting open the abdomen. The operation is performed with a sort of surgical telescope pushed through a small hole made in the abdomen. It is technically more difficult than ordinary sterilization and complications can arise. All forms of sterilization are best regarded as irreversible.

See also **pregnancy**; **vasectomy**

succubus

An evil female spirit who seeks sexual intercourse with sleeping men.

See also **incubus**

syphilis

A sexually transmitted disease which if left untreated can eventually lead to death. The symptoms develop approximately four weeks after contact with an infected person in the form of a sore, usually on the genitals, which ulcerates and eventually goes away. Syphilis can be completely cured by antibiotics, but if the infection remains untreated the germs can cause appalling and fatal symptoms, even decades later, and can be passed on by a woman to her children, causing deformities. Routine blood tests for syphilis are carried out on all expectant mothers.

See also **chancre**; **sexually transmitted disease**

T

tampon

A device made usually of a cotton mixture, small and tubular in shape, which is used internally in the vagina by women to mop up menstrual flow. Tampons are supplied with or without a cardboard or plastic applicator, and have a tag for easy removal.
See also **sanitary towel**; **toxic shock syndrome**

tart

Slang for a woman of easy virtue, or prostitute. It was originally a shortened form of the word *sweetheart*.
See also **prostitute**

testes

See **testicles**

testicles

The two male sex glands, which hang more or less side by side in the scrotum. Also known as *testes*, or **gonads**, (but commonly and descriptively called *balls* or *bollocks*), these glands manufacture sperms. An undescended testicle is one which is stuck in the canal that leads down from the abdomen (*cryptorchidism*), and a minor operation may be required to bring it down to avoid damage to fertility.
See also **cremasteric reflex**; **monorchism**; **scrotum**

test-tube baby

See *in vitro* **fertilization**

thrush

See **candida**

toxic shock syndrome

An infection of staphylococci originating from the vagina,

usually associated with the use of superabsorbent tampons. It is a rare condition, whose symptoms may include sudden collapse, with low blood pressure and shock. Women who have suffered toxic shock syndrome are advised not to use tampons or any vaginally inserted contraceptive devices. Tampon packets now carry warnings of the condition, as well as advice on how to avoid infection.
See also **tampon**

transsexual
A person who feels trapped in the wrong sex body. Unlike transvestites, transsexuals wear opposite-sex-clothes as an expression of their true gender, and may wish to have their bodies changed surgically, regardless of pain or expense.
See also **transvestite**

transvestite
A person who dresses in the clothes of the opposite sex; also known as a ***cross-dresser***. Transvestites include the heterosexual male who is sexually aroused by wearing women's underwear, and the 'drag queen' who wishes to look like a woman to attract other homosexual males.
See also **transsexual**

trichomoniasis
A common infection now listed as a **sexually transmitted disease**. Symptoms may occur in women but only rarely in men. There can be a vaginal discharge (in women), irritation, itching, pain during intercourse, and a mild burning during urination. Control of the infection is usually successful if both partners are treated.

trick
A colloquialism which, in the context of sexuality, usually refers to a 'one-night stand', an anonymous sexual encounter between two consenting homosexual males.
See also **homosexual**

U

urinary passage

See **urethra**

urethra

The urinary passage which leads to the bladder. In women this is situated between the vaginal opening and the clitoris. In men it is the same passage from which the sperms are ejaculated from the penis.

See also **Appendix**; **vagina**

uterus

The organ in a woman in which a baby is conceived and nourished until birth; also known as the ***womb***. It is shaped like a pear, and made up of a network of muscle fibres. These contract at special times within the menstrual cycle, at childbirth, when breastfeeding, and also, it is believed, during sexual stimulation of the nipples and at orgasm.

See also **endometritis; endometriosis**

V

vacuum pump

An aid to erection, in the form of an external device which applies vacuum pressure to the penis to force blood into its tissues. Considered unsafe, it can cause permanent damage to the genitals and urinary tract.
See also **penile implant**

vagina /vəˈdʒaɪnə/

The sexual passage or birth canal in the female from the uterus to the opening. The vagina is equipped with concertina-like muscles that encourage the male sperms on their journey to the uterus and, in childbirth, the baby on its way out into the world. The term comes from Latin, meaning 'sheath', and is so named because it is the receptacle for the penis during intercourse.
See also **vaginal infection**; **vaginal secretion**; **vaginismus**; **vaginitis**

vaginal infection

An infection which chiefly affects the vagina. The most common are the yeast infections such as candida (thrush) which cause a discharge and itching internally and externally, and can be treated with pessaries and creams. These and bacterial infections requiring antibiotics can be passed back and forth to a partner, and both need to be treated. It is not unusual for a woman to have two different types of infection at the same time, requiring different medication.
See also **sexually transmitted disease**

vaginal discharge

See **vaginal infection**; **vaginal secretion**

vaginal orgasm

See **orgasm**

vaginal secretion

Mucus from the cervix which bathes the vagina. These natural secretions keep the vagina moist and clean, change in substance and flow according to the monthly cycle, and are often copious during ovulation.

See also **menstruation**; **vagina**

vaginismus /vædʒɪnˈɪzmʊs/

A condition where a muscle spasm around the vagina makes intercourse painful or impossible. It can occur in women who are otherwise sexually active and able to reach orgasm through clitoral stimulation. It may be the result of a psychological block or a physical problem, such as attempting intercourse too soon after childbirth.

See also **intercourse, sexual**; **vagina**

vaginitis

A soreness or tenderness in the vagina. It is often caused by bruised tissues after over-enthusiastic or clumsy intercourse, but can also be the sign of a minor infection or a sexually transmitted disease.

See also **atrophic vaginitis**

vas deferens

See **vasectomy**

vasectomy

A popular form of male sterilization. It is performed under local anaesthetic by surgically cutting through the *vas deferens* (Latin 'deferent vessel', ie a vessel which 'carries down or out'), a duct which carries sperms from the testicles to the urethra. The operation does not normally affect virility, and seminal fluid will continue to be produced at orgasm. Vasectomy is best regarded as irreversible.

See also **penis**

vasocongestion

Increase of blood supply to the genitals and the female breasts. During sexual arousal vasocongestion causes erection of the penis and, in females, the expansion or *ballooning of the vagina* and the swelling of the genitals.

venal pleasures

Pleasures which may be bought; from Latin *venalis* 'that which is for sale'. The term usually refers to sexual favours from, for example, a prostitute.

venereal disease

See **sexually transmitted disease**

vibrator

A penis-shaped, often plastic device used for vaginal stimulation. It is usually battery operated, but if run off the mains electricity it must be earthed for safety reasons. It is not recommended for anal stimulation, as it can get lost and cause much embarrassment when it has to be removed surgically.
See also **artificial phallus**

virgin

A person, usually referring to a female, who has had no sexual intercourse. An unbroken hymen used to be considered proof of virginity in the 18th century, and even in some Mediterranean countries today a young woman is expected to bleed copiously on her wedding night. It is now known that the absence or presence of the hymen has nothing to do with proof of virginity.
See also **hymen**

voyeur /vwɑːˈjɛː/

A title given to someone who treats sex as a non-playing, spectator sport. The term is also commonly used for *peeping Toms* – men who get a kick out of secretly watching the opposite sex undressing, etc.
See also **fetishism**

vulva

The female external genitals. These are the sex organs which can actually be seen, including the inner and outer lips of the vagina, the vaginal opening, and the clitoris. Slang words abound for the female genitalia, and include the most forceful taboo word, *cunt*, as well as many milder forms such as *muffin*, *twat*, and *pussy*.

See also **genitalia**

W

wank
See **masturbation**

warts
See **human papillomavirus**

wet dream
See **nocturnal emission**

whore
See **prostitute**

withdrawal method
See **coitus interruptus**

womb
See **uterus**

X

XX and XY embryos

The human embryos. Most humans have 46 chromosomes, two of which are the sex chromosomes. 46XX is the normal female pattern, and 46XY the normal male pattern. Researchers have identified more than 70 abnormalities resulting from extra or missing chromosomes. (See also **embryo**.)

XY embryo

See **XX and XY embryos**

Y, Z

yeast infection
See **candida**

zygote
The fertilized egg. The single-cell zygote divides into cells and grows as it journeys towards the uterus. Four weeks after fertilization the collection of cells is called an ***embryo***, and becomes a ***foetus*** at eight weeks.
See also **embryo**; **foetus**.

Appendix

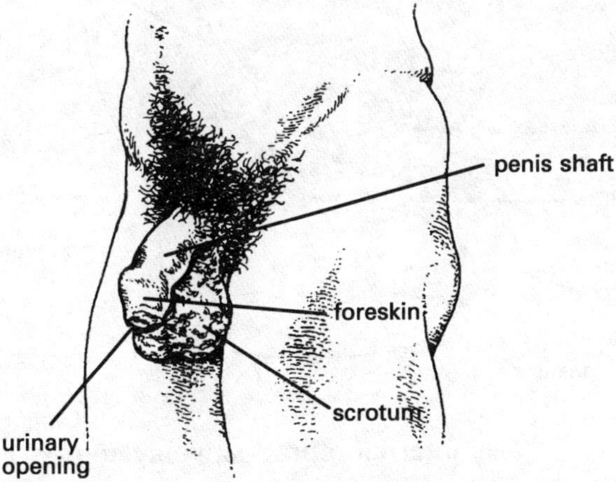

Uncircumcised penis

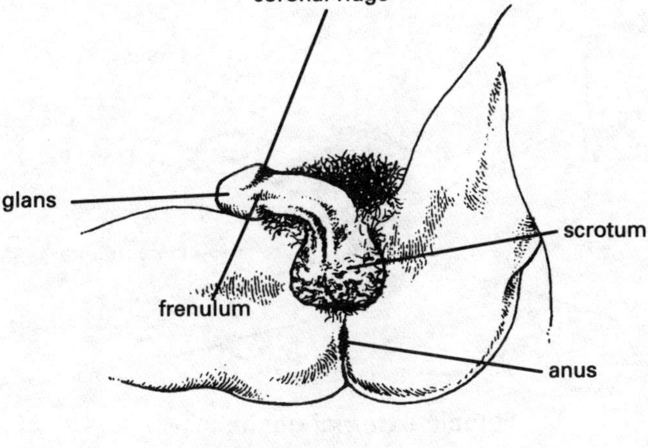

Circumcised penis

Appendix

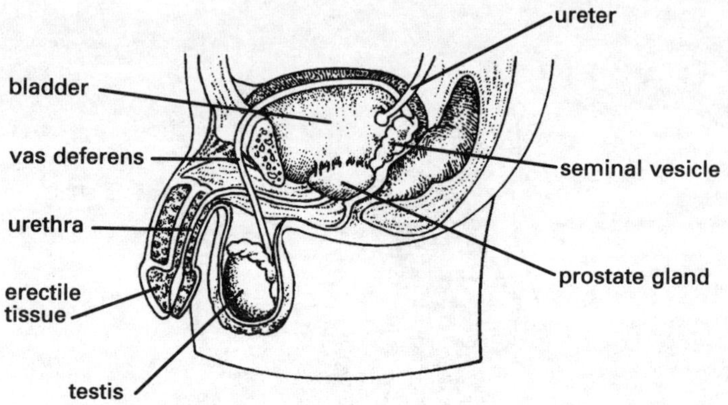

Male internal reproductive system

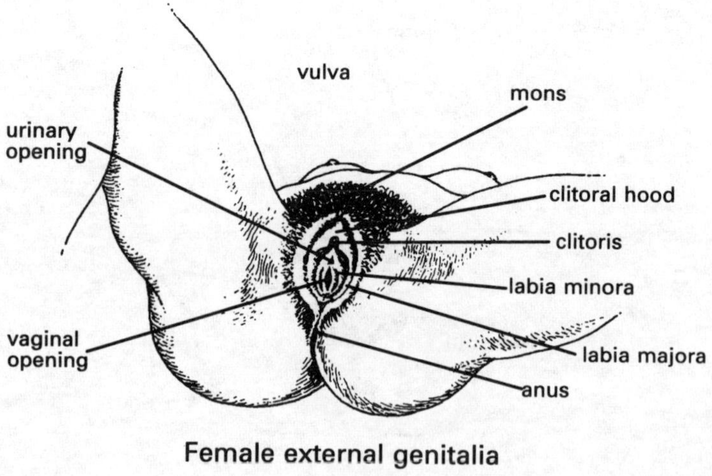

Female external genitalia

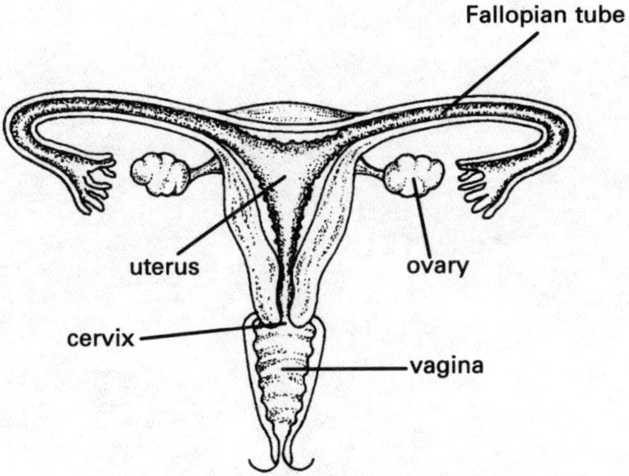

Female reproductive system